An Animal Family

TIGERS AND CUBS

By Emilia Hendrix

Gareth Stevens PUBLISHING

Please visit our website, www.garethstevens.com. For a free color catalog of all our high-quality books, call toll free 1-800-542-2595 or fax 1-877-542-2596.

Library of Congress Cataloging-in-Publication Data

Hendrix, Emilia, author.
Tigers and cubs / Emilia Hendrix.
pages cm. — (An animal family)
Includes index.
ISBN 978-1-4824-3791-1 (pbk.)
ISBN 978-1-4824-3792-8 (6 pack)
ISBN 978-1-4824-3793-5 (library binding)
1. Tiger—Juvenile literature. 2. Tiger—Behavior—Juvenile literature. I. Title.
QL737.C23H4575 2016
599.756—dc23
2015025061

First Edition

Published in 2016 by
Gareth Stevens Publishing
111 East 14th Street, Suite 349
New York, NY 10003

Editor: Ryan Nagelhout
Designer: Andrea Davison-Bartolotta

Photo credits: Cover, p. 1 Joel Sartore/Getty Images; p. 5 Photocech/Shutterstock.com; pp. 7, 24 (fur) andamanec/Shutterstock.com; pp. 9, 24 (stripe) Destinyweddingstudio/Shutterstock.com; pp. 11, 24 (streak) zhouyousifang/Getty Images; p. 13 apple2499/Shutterstock.com; p. 15 Zhiltsov Alexandr/Shutterstock.com; p. 17 (top left) Stefan Simmerl/Shutterstock.com; p. 17 (top right) Michal Ninger/Shutterstock.com; p. 17 (bottom left) Sarah Cheriton-Jones/Shutterstock.com; pp. 17 (bottom right), 19 Anan Kaewkhammul/Shutterstock.com; p. 21 George Lamson/Shutterstock.com; p. 23 Julian W/Shutterstock.com.

Printed in the United States of America

CPSIA compliance information: Batch #CW16GS: For further information contact Gareth Stevens, New York, New York at 1-800-542-2595.

Contents

Meet the Cats 4
Fur Stripes. 8
Big Streaks. 10
Cute Cubs 14
Words to Know 24
Index. 24

Tigers are big cats.

They have lots of hair.
This is called fur.

They have lines
in their fur.
These are stripes.

They live in groups.
These are
called streaks.

Some live in zoos.

Baby tigers are called cubs.

They are very cute.

Cubs cannot see
at first.

Their mother takes care of them.

She gives the cubs food. Later, she teaches them to hunt.

Words to Know

fur

streak

stripe

Index

cubs 14, 18, 22

fur 6, 8

streak 10

zoos 12